D0793441

THE
CLADDAGH
RING

THE
CLADDAGH
RING

Malachy McCourt

Running Press

PHILADELPHIA · LONDON

Library of Congress Control Number 2003104591

ISBN 0-7624-1708-0

This book may be ordered by mail from the publisher.
Please include $1.00 for postage and handling.
But try your bookstore first!

Running Press Book Publishers
125 South Twenty-second Street
Philadelphia, Pennsylvania 19103-4399

Log onto www.specialfavors.com to order Running Press®
Miniature Editions™ with your own custom-made covers!

Visit us on the web!
www.runningpress.com

TABLE OF CONTENTS

THERE IS IN Ireland a place called Claddagh, simply pronounced *Klada*, which nestles in close proximity to the sea and to the university city of Galway. A hardy breed of fisherfolk inhabit this little hamlet, having managed to maintain their odd individuality for many centuries. And when they've had to emigrate, they have always sought their own kin so that excessive use of language is not called for in everyday communication. How is it, then, that a ring—the Claddagh ring—is named after and will always be associated with this once remote and isolated fishing village? A ring so simple in its visual statement that the mere presentation of it to one's beloved takes away all need for words. The plain gold wedding cingulum indicates an eternity of attachment regardless of exigencies, whereas the Claddagh ring symbolically pledges not only everlasting love, but fealty, loyalty, trust, faith. Its motto, "Let love and friendship reign," is there to see in the sight of a heart being caressed by loving hands, and capstoned by a simple crown. There are many legends about the origins of the Claddagh ring's design and its Galway associations. It is said that the combination of hands, heart, and crown is the coat of arms of the Joyce family, and the famous James who may not have set foot in Galway did marry a native of the Claddagh region, one Nora Barnacle, thus getting close to his roots. Neither of these lovers were known to possess a ring, but other famous and infamous fools, clowns, hypocrites, and pseudo-Irish have been known to sport this pure symbol of love and friendship. Queen (we are not amused) Victoria proudly exhibited her ring made in Ireland even as millions of the misfortunate were dying of a man-induced starvation program. Her son Edward VII, it was said, was fond of this ring too. Other people in their millions can't wait to get a finger in their very own rings, particularly as it was bruited about that a bricklayer's daughter, Grace Kelly, who married a gambling casino operator, self-styled Prince Ranier, were showing off their rings to anyone who would look and listen. Wearing the ring didn't do much for Ronald Reagan, the forgetful president, and history will record the love lives of John F. Kennedy and Bill Clinton, who claim Irish heritage and love for the ring and its aura.

There seem to be no demarcation lines between the types of people who buy and wear and give this ring. It's fashionable among liars, loonies, rockers like U2, wild men like Oasis, actresses like Julia Roberts, Jennifer Aniston, and Mia Farrow, and now—get this—the rapper community have seized and are pledging their troth with an exchange of Claddagh rings.

As well as evoking noble sentiments from mature and spiritually exalted human beings, falling in love can also evoke drivel and doggerel from slobbery would-be poets and dreary sentimentality, enough to make a person vomit, and so the Irish do endure the likes of Galway Bay and the Old Claddagh Ring because the spirit of the ring makes it easy to forgive these atrocious insults to the Muse.

How the ring came to be a part of our history and lore, our life and love, is something of a mystery well worth exploring, and that's what this tome is about. It's a loving look at a loving and universal symbol of the best of the heart, the head, the hands, and the invisible soul of humanity. May your heart be clasped by the hands of your beloved, and may your days be crowned with happiness, and occasional bouts of ecstasy.

—Malachy McCourt
New York City
April 2003

ACKNOWLEDGMENTS

Thanks are due to Jonathan Margetts of T. Dillon & Sons—Galway's Original Makers of the Claddagh Ring (est. 1750), and his staff at The Claddagh Museum, for their assistance in the research for this book. I'd like to thank Tom Kenny of Kenny's Bookshop and Art Galleries Ltd. in Galway, and also Dorothy King, for their generous assistance as well. Several books were enormously valuable as sources for this book, most notably *Down by the Claddagh* by Peader O'Dowd, *Rain on the Wind* by Walter Macken, *The Claddagh Ring Story* by Cecily Joyce, *A History of Ireland* by Mike Cronin, and *The Story of the Claddagh Ring* by Sean McMahon.

THE OLD CLADDAGH RING

by *Patrick B. Kelly*

The old Claddagh ring, sure it was my
   grandmother's,
She wore it a lifetime and gave it to me;
All through the long years, she wore it so
   proudly,
It was made where the Claddagh rolls
   down to the sea.
What tales it could tell of trials and
   hardships,
And of grand happy days when the whole
   world could sing—
So away with your sorrow, it will bring
   love tomorrow,
Everyone loves it, the Old Claddagh Ring.

With the crown and the crest to remind
me of honour,
And clasping the heart that God's blessing
would bring,
The circle of gold always kept us
contented,
'Twas true love entwined in the Old
Claddagh Ring.
As she knelt at her prayers and thought
of her dear ones,
Her soft, gentle smile would charm a
king;
And on her worn hand as she told me
the story,
You could see the bright glint of the Old
Claddagh Ring.

It was her gift to me and it made me so
 happy,
With this on my finger my heart it would
 sing;
No king on his throne could be half so
 happy
As I am when I'm wearing my Old
 Claddagh Ring.
When the angels above call me up to
 heaven
In the heart of the Claddagh their voices
 will sing
Saying "Away with your sorrow, you'll be
 with us tomorrow,
Be sure and bring with you the old
 Claddagh Ring."

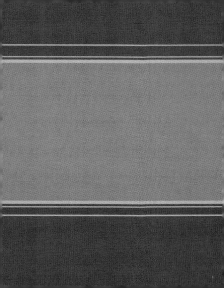

CHAPTER I

*When the angels above call
me up to heaven*

The Claddagh Heart Breaks

IT WAS JUST a day after the terrorist attacks on the World Trade Center in New York on September 11, with fires still burning beneath the rubble. All over Manhattan, scores of anxious people were taping pictures of their friends and loved ones on walls, subway stations, on the sides of phone booths; any available flat surface. Hundreds of photographs formed heartbreaking collages at many of these shrines, where people came to stare solemnly at the photographs of disappeared human beings of all ethnic groups and nationalities, and then drifted quietly away.

The faces, so full of life in these pictures, appeared with descriptions—brief details of their lives that managed to say so much. The fliers said everything, in fact. People stopped to read, but never for long, as grief overcame them. Beneath one photo of a man and his two young daughters was the message, "We love you daddy. Please come home." Another read, "Expecting first child this week." There were details about their clothes, where they were ("Last seen on 100th floor, helping co-workers near elevator bank"), and mention of scars, tattoos, and other distinguishing features.

For weeks and weeks, even after it became obvious that there would be no more rescues at Ground Zero, these signs remained posted around New York. The same faces looked out at us from walls or street lamps or trees, and they became familiar to us—almost like an acquaintance.

One detail that emerged again and again on these fliers was a reference to a certain piece of jewelry many of the missing persons were wearing at the time of this tragedy. "Irish Claddagh ring on left hand." This phrase, and variations of it, appeared on countless fliers—a reference to the Irish faith ring with the motto, "Let Love and Friendship Reign." As demographic study of the victims would later show, Irish Americans were heavily represented in those towers on September 11.

Jim Dwyer of the *New York Times*, in an article published on November 11, 2001, estimated that of the nearly 3,000 victims at the World Trade Center, one in five had traces of an Irish background. Dwyer wrote, "Among the surnames of the dead or missing are 12 Lynches, 10 Murphys, 9 Kellys, 5 Egans, 4 McCarthys, multiples of Kennedy, Sullivan, O'Brien, Gallagher. And so on."

In the days following the attack, friends and relatives of the victims filed thousands of missing persons reports with the American Red Cross, and those reports contain numerous mentions of Claddagh rings presumed to have been worn by the missing on that September day. Initial reports about the exact number of Claddagh rings recovered from Ground Zero reached mythic proportions. One such story that has spread across the globe concerns the parents of a missing firefighter who appeared at the site of the World Trade Center rescue operation shortly after the attacks and found the captain in charge of the shift. Perhaps, they told him, their son could be identified by a gold Claddagh ring he had been wearing. The captain, the story goes, had the solemn task of explaining to the heartbroken parents that so far, more than two hundred Claddagh rings had been recovered in the ruins of New York's majestic twin towers.

While people dispute the exact number of Claddagh rings recovered at Ground Zero, the rings do underscore the tragedy. In the days following the attack, Brian Cowen, the Irish foreign minister, appeared in New York to pay respects on behalf of the Irish citizenry. Dwyer reported, in his story in the *New York Times*, that after visiting Ground Zero, a shaken Cowen rode in an elevator at Police Headquarters with a police officer, who explained that in order to identify the missing and dead, family members had been asked to provide a list of personal items—and the Claddagh ring had turned up many times. According to Dwyer, the officer told Cowen that in the police and fire departments alone, "fifteen to twenty of the people we lost were wearing Claddagh rings."

New York's Finest and New York's Bravest, respectively the New York Police and Fire Departments, suffered devastating losses on September 11: twenty-three members of the NYPD, and 343 firemen. Aside from Cantor Fitzgerald, the bond brokerage house that lost 658 employees, the FDNY lost more lives than any other department or company.

Traditionally, Irish Americans have gravitated toward these civil service departments in significant numbers for generations—and fighting New York City fires has long been at the core of the Irish American way of life. In the earliest years of the United States, volunteers formed the corps of firefighting until it became obvious, mostly due to urban development and growth, that full-time firefighters were

a necessity. It wasn't until the end of
the Civil War that New York City
formed a professional firefighting
force, which coincided with the boat-
loads of Irish immigrants who fled
genocidal starvation in Ireland and
arrived at Ellis Island in tremendous
numbers. Because the Irish could
speak English, they had an advantage
over other groups of immigrants, such
as the Germans and the Italians. The
Irish had already been making significant political inroads, helping them to

secure jobs in public works projects. It did not hurt that some of the bravest soldiers in the Civil War were members of the "Fire Zouaves," a legendary Irish regiment consisting of mostly volunteer firemen from New York City who fought valiantly at Bull Run near Manassas Junction, Virginia, while overwhelmingly outnumbered by Confederate troops. Despite taking hundreds of casualties, the Zouaves withstood a charge by legendary cavalry commander J.E.B. Stuart, and then fell in with another heavily Irish regiment—the 69th from New York. When the Southerners seized the 69th's green regimental flag, the Fire Zouaves advanced into heavy fire and recaptured it.

The earliest New York City firefighters were criminal/political gangs who sometimes fought each other for the privledge of fighting fires. See Herbert Asbury's *Gangs of New York*.

This spirit continued in the early years of the Fire Department of New

York, in which the Irish played a major role. Firefighting is perhaps nowhere more dangerous than in New York— where the unofficial motto has been and continues to be, "fight every fire." From 1865 to 1905, one hundred firemen were killed in the line of duty, and two-thirds of those were Irish. Over the years, an influx of new ethnic groups have made the FDNY more representative of the city's diversity, but as evidenced on September 11, 2001, the Irish have still been gravitat-

ing to firefighting in heavy numbers.
What is also clear is that the bravery
demonstrated by those fighting
Zuoaves at Bull Run represents a spirit
of heroism and courage that has never
wavered in the ranks of the FDNY;
and the strength of that legacy reaches
across ethnic divides. A hundred firefighters had been killed in action up
to September 11. More than 135
years, and one day twice that number
were wantonly done to death.

The fact that so many firefighters

were wearing Claddagh rings on what turned out to be their last day on earth is proof that what the ring stands for (love, loyalty, and friendship) resonates as strongly now as it has for generations. For the Claddagh ring is no stranger to tragedy, and September 11 was not the first day in history where the hand that wore it met death.

The year was 1845, and the population of Ireland had been growing rapidly over sixty years—exploding to eight million from just three million in the late 1770s. British laws had put a limit on the amount of land Catholics could own, creating smaller plots of land for much of the Irish population to farm. With these small plots, the people relied heavily on the potato crop for subsistence-level farming, and the only way the population could produce enough food on these sub-acre plots was to grow potatoes.

The first signs of a problem appeared in England in the summer of 1845, when a fungus was identified in a potato, leading to a blight. Potato harvests across Europe began to fail, and by fall of that year, the blight had spread to Ireland. A black rot had blanketed the country, destroying any hopes for a bumper crop, and the peasantry found their potatoes rotting in the fields. The economic impact was immediate and devastating, as the people had nothing to pay their British and Protestant landlords for rent. Crop after crop produced no food for six years, and landlords began evicting their tenants. Those who continued to eat the rotten tubers sickened quickly, and before long, entire regions of Ireland grew infested with cholera and typhus.

Thousands upon thousands of peasants underwent removal into workhouses, where they succumbed to disease and starvation. The lucky ones got money from their landlords or through government-sponsored projects to emigrate, and waves of poor and ravaged Irish began to flee in "coffin ships" to America. The poorest, of course, had little choice but to stay behind and accept their fate, and statistically, nowhere was the suffering worse than in western Ireland—particularly Connaught, where the rate of death was five times higher than in many other counties.

Those peasants without the money to set sail for America, often abandoned their land and set off on foot in a desperate search for food, taking other diseases such as typhoid and dysentery with them and spreading them to wider areas of the country. Villages such as Claddagh, the small fishing community in Galway, were able to keep starvation at bay, but they were not able to avoid the cholera that devastated the region.

From 1845 to 1850, over a million lives were lost from starvation and disease, and emigration depleted the population in Ireland to just five million. In 1906, William Dillon, owner of Dillon's, the Galway jeweler, wrote an article entitled "The 'Claddagh' Ring" which appeared in the *Galway Archaeological and Historical Journal*. In the article, Dillon tells a story told to him by a Galway pawnbroker named John Kirwan, who noted that during the Irish famine, people of Claddagh had pawned their gold Claddagh rings for an advance of cash so that they could leave Ireland. Dillon wrote:

Mr. Kirwan seeing no prospect of them being ever redeemed,

realized his money by selling them as old gold to be broken up and consigned to the melting-pot. The 'Claddagh' ring was not at that time the fashionable ring which it is now, and there being no purchasers, these fine old rings, many of them being the rare old G.R. rings now valued for 5 pounds each, were consigned to the melting-pot at the comparatively low price to be obtained for old gold. The fact is that the Claddagh population was at this time greatly reduced, hundreds going to the USA, where to the present day there exists a colony of them, at Boston, called Claddagh, after their ancestral village.

There is no telling, of course, how many Claddagh rings were displaced from their owners during the Famine. The tradition of passing them down a generation surely continued as people starved or became ill, and as Dillon noted in his story a hundred years ago, all sentimentality vanished in the fight for survival. As the Irish fled the Connemara region where disease and hunger were the most severe, many of them no doubt traveled with Claddagh rings, which, in turn, makes them familiar to oustide people.

Claddagh rings began turning up at Ellis Island during the mass exodus from Ireland in the 19th century, as shiploads of Irish came over with little more than the clothes on their backs. It's realistic to assume, given the numbers of Irish who perished aboard those "coffin ships," that a great many emigrants, with dreams of a better life in America, took their last breath of air with a Claddagh ring upon their finger. These rings were no doubt passed on to relatives and loved ones aboard those ships—in contrast to the tradition mentioned in the poem by Patrick B. Kelly, where a grandmother

difference between fact and fiction often blurs what is truly known. Yet the remarkable thing is that despite the obvious elements rooted in mythology, the facts that are known about the ring are fascinating with little or no embellishment.

Claddagh rings began turning up at Castle Garden in New York, where millions of immigrants entered the United States before Ellis Island opened in 1892.

The history of the Claddagh ring

abounds in mystery and myth with the result that the giver or presenter of this treasure feels as if he or she is involving the beloved recipient in a romantic conspiracy. Every one of the givers has a story of the origins of this symbol with the fact and fiction interwoven so that the real story is never to be known. Does it matter? Well, the real story is as romantic as one can get, so read on! ❧

CHAPTER II

And on her worn hand she told me the story

The Claddagh Ring Stories

TWO TALES CLAIM to explain the origins of the Claddagh ring. Both involve the Joyce family of Galway. Of the two stories, the tale of Margaret Joyce, or "Margaret of the Bridges" as she became known, has always appealed to the most romantic at heart. Margaret lived in sixteenth-century Galway, and as fortune would have it, a chance encounter with a Spanish merchant would forever change her life. Not only did she meet the alleged man of her dreams while up to her ankles in water alongside a riverbank where she did the family's laundry, but the man apparently fell in love at first sight. And he was quite wealthy. A marriage quickly followed, and so Margaret Joyce soon became Margaret de Rona, wife of Domingo de Rona, who, almost immediately after marrying the young Margaret, whisked her off to Spain on one of his ships. However, the honeymoon would not last long. Domingo was not a young man, and the suddeness of married life may have been a bit too much of a strain on the elderly Spaniard's heart. In short, Domingo died soon after their return to Spain, and now Margaret de Rona was a young widow with a newly inherited fortune.

Life in Spain, however, did not agree with the homesick Margaret, and after getting her affairs in order, she quickly set sail for Ireland. Too young and too rich to stay a widow for long, Margaret married Oliver Og ffrench, the mayor of Galway, in 1596, and strangely, he set out for a voyage of his own, leaving Margaret at home and apparently restless. Rich and bored are two words that usually do not coincide with significant contributions to mankind. Margaret, however, was inspired to pass the time and spend her money in a manner that the people of western Ireland have greatly appreciated, according to the legend. At her own expense, she began building bridges all over Connaught. It is not clear what her husband, Mayor ffrench, must have thought when he first learned of his wife's little "hobby" while away. Perhaps he didn't mind so much, as this ambitious public works project (which would cost his constituents nothing in taxes!) was sure to help him in his next election campaign. Still, it must have been quite a shock to the ffrench checking account! Countless stone bridges were erected across the Connemara region, with Margaret going from site to site, overseeing much of the work done by masons. Strange as this was, it would only get stranger.

Legend has it that Margaret, while sitting down at one particular bridge project during construction, was visited by a large eagle bearing a gift. In her lap, the eagle dropped the golden prototype of the Claddagh ring as a gift from God for Margaret's charity and good works.

Historians recount different versions with details varying over time, but the general theme of the tale remains. Hardiman, in his book, *The History of the Town and County of Galway*, written in 1820, wrote of the story of Margaret in great detail:

Heaven was again propitious to another of this family; Margaret Joyes, great grand daughter of the above named William, who was surnamed, Margaret na Drehide, Margaret of the Bridges, from the great number which she built. The story of this singular woman is still current amongst her descendants. They relate she was born of reduced but genteel parents and was first married to Domingo de Rona, a wealthy Spanish merchant, who traded to Galway, where he fell in love with, and married her; and soon after departing for Spain, died there, leaving her mistress of an immense property. Upon his decease, having no issue by him, she married Oliver Oge ffrench, who was Mayor of Galway in 1596. So far the narrative is probable and consistent, but what follows will try the credulity of the reader. It relates that this lady, during the absence of her second husband, on a voyage, erected most part of the bridges of the Province of Connaught, at her own expense! And that she was one day sitting before the workmen, when an eagle, flying over her head, let fall into her bosom, a gold ring adorned with a brilliant stone, the nature of which no lapidary could ever discover. It was preserved by her descendants, as a most valuable relique in 1661 (the date of the MS from which this account is taken) as a mark supposed to have been sent from Heaven of its approbation of her good works and charity. This fable though still piously believed, by some of this family, was humorously ridiculed by Latocnaye, an incredulous French traveller, who visited Galway about the end of the last century.

The Frenchman Hardiman referred to was none other than Le Chavalier de la Tocnaye, who traveled around Ireland on a walking tour, and wrote about it in his book, *Promenade d'un francais dans l'Irlande,* published in

1797. In true French fashion, de la Tocnaye could not help ridiculing the Irish for their fondness for such tales, as is obvious from the following passage from his book:

It is said also that thirteen families, whose names are still common, laid the city's foundations, and tradition avers that, while a good lady of the name of Joyce watched the masons who built Galway Bridge at her expense, an eagle dropped a chain of gold in her lap, and placed a crown on her head. The gold chain is still preserved by the Joyce family according to the story told to me. The people have always loved fables—had Galway become a Rome this one would certainly have been believed.

It turns out, de la Tocnaye had a great deal to say about Galway and not all of it is condescending. But we'll come back to that later. Margaret of the Bridges is the lady who commands our attention at the moment. Nearly 200 years ago, she commanded the attention of one Caesar Otway, author of the book, *A Tour in Connaught*, published in 1839. If de la Tocnaye demonstrated a bit of skepticism toward the tale of Margaret and her dalliance with the giant bird of prey that came bearing gifts, Otway did the exact opposite. He swallowed the tale, hook-line-and-sinker, and even dared to embellish it, colorfully describing the scene as if he had stumbled into the stream himself, and with paper and pen, recorded the events for all the world to enjoy.

De la Tocnaye wrote that Margaret, the daughter of John Joyce, was out one day washing clothes in a stream off the River Corrib, when who should gallantly ride by but Don Domingo de Rona, the wealthy Biscayan merchant. De Rona had come to Galway with "a barrack" of Benecarlo wine, an ingredient in high demand by the local merchants who were famous for "doctoring the claret" with their own custom concoctions. De la Tocnaye describes Margaret working away in the stream with toes "as straight and fair as her fingers, not a corn or bunnion on one of them" as she washed the family linen. "The don," he wrote, "was captivated with the maid; he made love as Spaniards do; produced proofs of his pedigree, and his cash, and in due time they were married, and proceeded to Corunna."

However, not long after the marriage, de Rona died (for he was no spring chicken at the time of his dalliances with fair Margaret) and "Donnade Rona" came back to Ireland a "sparkling and wealthy widow." De la Tocnaye noted that one Oliver Og ffrench took a liking to Margaret upon her return, and after a more lengthy courtship, the two eventually married.

Then ffrench became mayor of Galway and one of the most successful merchants in the city—and was not above engaging himself in the popular Galway tradition of smuggling restricted goods overseas. Meanwhile, Margaret, a.k.a. Donna Domingo de Rona ffrench by this time, was idle by no means. De la Tocnaye then describes the sequence of events as she set out to become the "greatest improver in the west" by engaging in her passion for building bridges:

She might have made as good a pontifex at Pope Joan, and heaven's blessing was on her for her good works; for one day as she was superintending her masons, an eagle came soaring from the ocean, and balancing itself with poised wing just over the dame, it dropped at her feet a ring formed of a single stone, so strange and outlandish in its make and form, but yet so beautiful and so precious that, though the most skilful lapidarires admired it, and would have given any price for it, none could say of what kind it was, or of what country or age was the workmanship; it has been kept in the family since. I wish I could tell the reader which of the Joyces now owns this precious relic. All I can say is, that it is not on the finger of big Jack, or his wife. But indeed the Joyces seem to have been a favoured race; it is a favour that they should be named and known as merry; for he who has 'a merry hath a continual feast'. I assume it to be a favour also that they were under the especial patronage of eagles.

Whether a crown was also placed on Margaret's head, or a "brilliant stone" placed in her lap, or whether she simply received the prototype of the Claddagh ring itself as a gift for her good works, is a detail that depends on the storyteller. In most versions, however, the design of the Claddagh ring was preserved by the Joyce family from 1661, thanks to the eagle and Margaret's passion for bridge building. Realistically, many of the elements of the Margaret story are rooted in Greek mythology, folklore, and fairytales common throughout Europe.

For instance, the great Greek dramatist, Aeschylus (525-456 B.C.),

author of *Prometheus Bound* and *Oresteia*
and widely considered the father of
Greek tragedy, was also inextricably
(and tragically) linked to the giant
bird. Not only did Aquila the eagle
play an important part in *Prometheus
Bound*, meting out Zeus's punishment
by continually swooping down on
Prometheus each dawn, pecking at his
liver, but Aeschylus found himself at
the mercy of such a bird. Lore has it
that an eagle, soaring overhead, mis-
took Aeschylus's head for a stone, and

dropped a tortoise on it, killing the dramatist instantly.

It is possible that de la Tocnaye, in his sarcastic gibe about Margaret's eagle, may have had another eagle from ancient Rome in mind. The legend goes that Roman engineers were surveying plans to make ancient Troy the capital of the Eastern Empire. Suddenly, an eagle swooped down and seized the measuring line from the engineers, dropping it in Byzantium, thereby redefining the capital.

Margaret Joyce, a.k.a. Margaret de Rona, a.k.a. Margaret French, a.k.a. Margaret of the Bridges, has been depicted in countless paintings and portrayed in numerous stories pertaining to the mysteries of the Claddagh ring's origin. Whether or not a swooping eagle descended from the skies over Connaught to bestow a ring, a stone and a crown upon the head of fair Margaret is not at issue here. Rather, the allure and the mystery of the tale is almost secondary to how it, and the design of the Claddagh ring, were preserved in a tiny, secluded fishing village in County Galway for so many years. For the history of the village of Claddagh is every bit as intriguing as how Margaret of the Bridges came to hold the secret of the Claddagh design.

Not as mystical, but just as intriguing, is the tale of Richard Joyce, who holds the key to the second story of the origin of the ring.

In 1675, Richard Joyce, a native of Galway, was on his way to the West Indies presumably aboard some type of merchant vessel. Adding to the usual danger of a sea voyage in those days was the constant threat of pirate ships. Corsairs, under Ottoman protection, dominated the Mediterranean seas, most notably along waters of North Africa, known as the "Barbary Coast." Manning these ships were Muslim pirates from Algeria, Morocco, Tunisia, and other states, authorized by their government to raid and plunder commercial ships trading with Christian countries. They disrupted trade in the region so skillfully that even Great Britain, with the world's most powerful navy, could not stop them. In fact, the Corsairs had begun to expand operations to the Atlantic, and were known to attack ships and towns from the Caribbean to the uppermost parts of North America.

Unfortunately for Richard Joyce, the pirates who raided his vessel were not only interested in the typical pirate booty of currency, food, and whatever else a ship might contain. The Algerian privateers were noted for capturing and enslaving passengers from these vessels. Some of them were sold, others transported and enslaved in Algeria. For almost fifteen years, until his release in 1689, Richard Joyce was a captive in Algeria, purchased by a successful Turkish goldsmith. It was during this time that Joyce apparently learned and mastered the craft that would ultimately gain him considerable wealth. Once again, James Hardiman, in his book, *The History of the Town and County of Galway* of 1820, describes Joyce's ordeal and release in the following manner:

Several individuals of this name have long felt grateful to the memory of William III, from the following circumstance, on the accession of that monarch to the throne of England. One of the first acts of his reign was to send an ambassador to Algiers, to demand the immediate release of all the British subjects detained there in slavery. The dey and council, intimidated, reluctantly complied with this demand. Among those released was a young man of the name of Joyes, a native of Galway, who fourteen years before, was captured on his passage to the West Indies, by an Algerine Corsair; on his arrival at Algiers, he was purchased by a wealthy Turk who followed the profession of a goldsmith, and who observing his slave, Joyes, to be tractable and ingenious, instructed him in his trade in which he speedily became an adept. The Moor, as soon as he heard of his release, offered him, in case he should remain, his only daughter in marriage, and with her half his property, but all these, with other tempting and advantageous proposals, Joyes resolutely declined.

Joyce returned to Galway, married, and ultimately became one of Ireland's most renowned goldsmiths. He brought back to Ireland not only a skill that was honed abroad (albeit in some trying circumstances) but also a style that was unique to the country and steeped in Moorish influence. He produced many silver chalices and other artifacts in this vein, but it was his rings, with the heart, the hands, and the crown, that captured the imagination of generations. Fortunately, many of the rings Joyce produced upon returning from Algeria survive today and bear his initials and marks. These are the oldest known Claddagh rings in existence, and are no doubt the reason so many are willing to believe that the origin of the Claddagh ring's design can be attributed to Richard Joyce—the young man captured by

Algerian Corsairs, and put to work by a master goldsmith.

While the tale of Margaret Joyce and her acquisition of the Claddagh ring is romantic enough to endure over the years, her story pretty much ends at the bridge after the visit by the eagle. Richard Joyce, on the other hand, continues to be a focal point for historians, as more details emerge of his work with Claddagh rings in Galway. What is most fascinating about his story is how a tiny and mysterious fishing village made the Claddagh ring its own after Joyce stopped producing them circa 1737. The history of this peaceful community along Galway Bay only adds to the allure, the charm, and the mystery of the Claddagh ring.

CHAPTER III

*'Twas true love entwined in the old
Claddagh ring*

Let Love and Friendship Reign

To understand just how the Claddagh ring may have developed, whether or not you choose to believe either of the romantic stories of Margaret and Richard, it is important to understand the origins of rings and the purposes for wearing them. In his book, *Rings for the Finger* (J.B. Lippincott Company, 1917), author George Frederick Kunz explains some of the earliest recognition of the ring as a bonding symbol:

The origin of the ring is some-
what obscure, although there is
good reason to believe that it is
a modification of the cylindri-
cal seal which was first worn
attached to the neck or to the
arm and was eventually
reduced in size so that it could
be worn on the finger.

. . . In his *Natural History*,
Pliny related the Greek fable of
the origin of the ring. For his
impious daring in stealing fire

from heaven for mortal man,
Prometheus had been doomed
by Jupiter to be chained for
30,000 years to a rock in the
Caucasus, while a vulture fed
upon his liver. Before long,
however, Jupiter relented and
liberated Prometheus; never-
theless, in order to avoid a vio-
lation of the original judg-
ment, it was ordained that the
Titan should wear a link of his
chain on one of his fingers as a

ring, and in this ring was set a fragment of the rock to which he had been chained, so that he might be still regarded as bound to the Caucasian knot.

It is interesting that Kunz mentions the knot as these were known for being an early favorite charm in primitive times—a piece of knotted cord or wire would be twisted into a knot. Kunz continues:

Frequently this was used to cast a spell over a person, so as to deprive him of the use of one of his limbs or one of his faculties: at other times, the power of the charm was directed against the evil spirit which was supposed to cause disease or lameness, and in this case the charm had curative power. It has been conjectured that the magic virtues attributed to rings originated in this way, the ring being regarded as a simplified form of a knot; indeed, not infrequently rings were and are made in the form of knots. This symbol undoubtedly signified the binding or attaching of the spell to its object, and the same idea is present in the true-lovers' knot.

If the origins of the Claddagh ring are swathed in intrigue, mystery, and folklore, the meaning of the ring is clear. Its motto, "Let Love and

Friendship Reign," is represented by three distinct symbols joined in unity on the ring. As we know, the hands signify faith in friendship, the crown loyalty, and the heart signifies love. In Gaelic, the phrase *Gra Dilseacht, agus Cairdeas*, pronounced phonetically as *Gra Deelshocked, ogis Kordiss,* means "Love, Loyalty, and Friendship." But the phrase, "Let Love and Friendship Reign" is the most commonly accepted translation of the meaning of the Claddagh ring.

There have been countless interpretations over the years, as author Cecily Joyce points out in her 1990 book, *The Claddagh Ring Story*. Joyce notes that the hands signify faith, trust or "plighted troth," and the heart not only includes love but charity. The crown, along with loyalty, may symbolize honor or "hope of future glory." Then, of course, there is the poem, which makes it all easy to remember!

The hands are there for friendship,
The heart is there for love.
For loyalty throughout the year,
The crown is raised above.

More mythical in nature, one Celtic interpretation has *Dagda*, of *Dagda-Mor*, the powerful father of the gods, representing the right hand of the ring. It was *Dagda* who had the ability to stop the sun in its place, which he once did for nine straight months according to legend. The mother of the Celts was known as *Danu* or *Anu* and represented the left hand, while *Beathauile*, not a person or a god but "life," is represented by the crown. The heart in this translation represents each and every person of mankind.

Yet another interpretation of the meaning of the ring corresponds to the Shamrock, which is one of the most ancient symbols of the Trinity among the Irish. The crown is interpreted as the Father, the left hand is the Son, and the right hand is the Holy Ghost, all of whom care for all of humanity, represented by the heart.

Despite the many variations of Claddagh ring designs, the presence of the hands, the heart, and the crown are what separate it from other "fede" or faith rings of ancient times. However, what is most uncommon about the Claddagh ring is the manner in which it can be worn. There is no telling how far these customs go back in time, and evidence would suggest that these options are more modern in practice, rather than ancient tradition. And yet, the very fact that people abide by them seriously when they get a Claddagh Ring is proof that the mystical nature of the ring is quite powerful and compelling.

Wearing the ring on the right hand with the crown turned inward to the wrist and the heart turned outward, indicates that your heart has not yet been taken. Wearing it on your right hand with the crown turned outward and the heart turned inward, indicates that you have made a commitment to someone. Wearing the Claddagh ring on your left hand with the crown turned outward and the heart turned inward, is an announcement that you have said "I do" and "I will" to your beloved.

While the significance of how the ring is worn may be more of a modern conception, fede rings, or "truth" rings, have been around since ancient Greek and Roman times, if not earlier.

Fede rings usually featured two hands clasped together, and Roman examples have been dated back to 4 A.D. It was also believed that the Romans were the first to begin wearing these rings on the third or "ring" finger of the left hand. The Romans even coined the phrase *vena amoris*, which means "vein of love" and comes from the Egyptian theory that this "vein" led directly to the heart.

CHRISTIANITY IN IRELAND

St. Patrick is the missionary who gets most of the credit for cultivating and spreading Christianity throughout Ireland, and while many historians believe that his missions may have been embellished and exaggerated, his contribution to Irish culture simply cannot be understated. Very little is known about Patrick. According to his "Confession," he was born in the early 400s A.D. in Roman Britain, probably in northern England, where his mother was a Gaul and his father an official with some family means. When Patrick was about sixteen, he was kidnapped, probably by Saxon or Pict raiders, and taken to Ireland where he was sold into slavery. It is believed that as a slave, he tended to sheep, possibly in Mayo or Sligo, and it was during this time in captivity that Patrick began praying, which continued for several years until he managed to escape.

Patrick is believed to have walked hundreds of miles across Ireland to the east coast, and then secured a spot on a ship to France (Gaul) where he began his training in earnest as a priest. According to his "Confession," he heard the call in his dreams, perhaps from God, to return to Ireland in 432, and he began roaming the Emerald Isle preaching the Gospel. Ireland at this time was holding many Celtic Pagan festivals, and Patrick set out to "Christianize" the masses—setting up churches and introducing religious order wherever he went—ultimately putting in place the Irish Church.

Along with Christianity, the production of books flourished in Ireland—replacing centuries of oral tradition, though some would argue that tradition has never wavered in the least! But the advent and proliferation of the written word in Ireland in the years following St. Patrick's return is considered one of the greatest contributions to civilization. The best known manuscript from this time is the Book of Kells—handwritten copies of the

Bible and other books written about 700 A.D. and illuminated by monks in Irish monasteries. Beautifully illuminated in painstakingly detail, the Book of Kells is currently housed at Trinity College in Dublin.

At around the same time the monks were busy documenting and transcribing the word of God in these ornate manuscripts, the Gaels began arriving in Ireland *en masse*, having already spread across most of Europe. Like most conquering peoples, the

Gaels brought with them their own cultural beliefs and established a new power structure in Ireland, but they also assimilated—intermarrying and establishing alliances within local and regional areas.

The fact that the Romans did not invade the Gaelic island had both advantages and disadvantages for the Irish culture. While it's true that the many Gaelic traditions have been preserved over centuries because they were never corrupted by Roman control, the country never witnessed many of the technological, agricultural, and military advances enjoyed by most European cultures after Roman conquest. Ireland became something of a safe haven for the cultivation of Christianity, and as the rest of Europe began to destruct under Roman rule, Ireland remained stable and even thrived as displaced scholars and intellectuals fled Europe. In short, Ireland did not experience Europe's dark ages, and later, when Christianity began to spread back to

Europe, it was launched from the solid base of Ireland.

Joan Evans, in her book, *English Jewelry from the Fifth Century A.D. to 1800* (Methuen & Co. Ltd., 1921), explained this cultural impact in terms of art and scholarship. She wrote that Ireland became a European center of Christianity, and intellectual minds "flocked like bees" to Irish centers of study such as Durrow and Armagh. As these centers of study flourished, Celtic art acquired a new importance in Irish culture, Evans noted, as manu-scripts, illuminated by "parchment and quill," eventually led to similar decorative patterns appearing in stone and metal arts of the time. Evans wrote:

Regular compartments and open recessed panels were filled with exquisite interlaced work, and zoomorphic patterns of lacertine monsters and long-billed birds. The rich and varied ornament was controlled by

a strong sense of line, propor-
tion and relief; the ancient traditions of pagan Celtic art
remained too strong for any
barbarian roughness to survive
in the refinement of the
Christian Celtic style.

The Irish artists demonstrated such
skill that samples of their work spread
to Europe, and before long, it was
known that the very best craftsmen of
the ninth century, according to Evans,

"came from the Irish foundation of St. Gall." It was very clear that some of the most common symbols in Christian Celtic art—such as the trumpet, the animal, and the spiral—symbols often seen in the ornate manuscripts of the time, inspired goldsmiths as well. It was then, Evans wrote, that artists created the Ardagh chalice, Bell-shrines, and the popular penannular brooches "to represent the magnificence and beauty of Christian Celtic metal work."

The penannular brooch is most notable. Evans believed that these jeweled pieces, which were common in Ireland and Scotland, were probably derived from a "pin with a wire bent in a circle through the head." The penannular brooch is unique in that the ring has a break in it (indicative of its name) and this pin is longer than the diameter of the ring. The wearer of the brooch would insert the pin into a pinched piece of the clothing or fabric so that it would pass between two points, then pull the pin through the break in the ring and turn. This would keep the brooch in place and secure it to the article of clothing. Evans also noted that the origins of many of these brooches have an element that could indeed be viewed as inspirational in design to the ring that would begin to appear centuries later:

The penannular form is found at an early date in Ireland. Some VI century examples are of comparatively small size, and have the ends of the ring terminating in birds' heads. Later the finials became broader and flatter, and so shaped that only their outside edge conforms to a circle. These finials are often shewn issuing from the mouths of birds' heads, as in the silver-gilt ring of a penannular brooch of about 800 in the museum of the Royal Irish Academy. This shews the tendency to close the ring and make it only an ornamental appendage of the pin, which arose as soon as the decoration of the brooch became of more importance than its practical use.

These brooches from the sixth century have all the key ingredients of what would later become the Claddagh Ring, and it does not require much imagination to see where goldsmiths made the leap from bird's heads to two hands clasping a heart in these brooches. As Evans noted, development of the ring brooch that would appear in the later years of the 14th century was probably used as a love-token, with two clasped hands often holding a stone. A development of the ring brooch that arose in the later years of the 14th century, probably used as a love-token, has two tiny clasped hands, sometimes holding a stone, projecting from the ring.

In her book, Evans noted that marriage rings from the Middle Ages were different from ornamental rings only by their posy—the sentimental inscription on either the inner or outer portion of a ring. She also noted that "clasped hands are often found on betrothal rings, both gimmel and of the ordinary shape; one in the British Museum is inscribed on the shoulders with the posy 'God Help,' and is chased at the back with a heart and two quatrefoil flowers rising from it."

It is also thought that Celtics during the Middle Ages cut and braided human hair, wrapped it around a finger or a wrist and wore it as a symbol of commitment. The "Gimmel" or "bond ring" was another ring of similar symbolism, as it consisted of two or sometimes three hoops that attached to the base of the ring. When worn around a finger, its appearance was that of a regular ring, but some historians have suggested that these rings may have been separated during the actual marriage ceremony as part of the vows of traditional union.

The Claddagh ring has come to represent more than just a betrothal ring. Grandmothers continue to give them to granddaughters as gifts whether or not a wedding is in the works. Grooms have been known to present them to their best men, and friends present them as friendship rings. Yet the rebirth and popularization of traditional Irish weddings around the world has led to a younger

generation's appreciation for the ring that states, "Let Love and Friendship Reign."

This book has been bound using
handcraft methods and
Smyth-sewn to ensure durability.

The dust jacket and
interior were designed by
SERRIN BODMER.

The text was edited by
MICHAEL WASHBURN.

The text was set in
BEMBO.

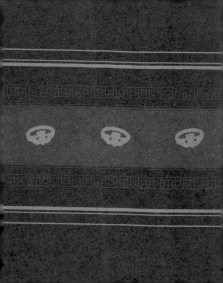